IMAGES
of England

WATFORD
THE SECOND SELECTION

Ballard's Buildings

7.6.1905

New Street, near St Mary's church, photographed by Whitford Anderson in 1905. The entrance to the overcrowded court known as Ballard's Buildings is just behind the figures on the pavement, while in the foreground William Day's sign invites travellers to his lodging house.

IMAGES
of England

WATFORD
THE SECOND SELECTION

Compiled by
Judith Knight

First published 1999
Copyright © Judith Knight, 1999

Tempus Publishing Limited
The Mill, Brimscombe Port,
Stroud, Gloucestershire, GL5 2QG

ISBN 0 7524 1136 5

Typesetting and origination by
Tempus Publishing Limited
Printed in Great Britain by
Midway Clark Printing, Wiltshire

On 10 May 1902 Princess Beatrice laid the memorial stone at the Royal Caledonian Asylum in Bushey, and the inhabitants of Watford and Bushey turned out *en masse* to see her travel through the High Street in Lord Hyde's carriage. The train carrying the royal party had left Euston at three o'clock and 'soon after half past it steamed into Watford Junction', where she was given a chair on the platform while being greeted by representatives of the Council. Previously it was thought that this photograph was of the visit by King Edward VII in 1909, but all the evidence shows that he travelled by car.

Contents

The elegant premises of Sun Printers in Whippendell Road. The company pioneered many colour printing techniques, largely under the direction of David Greenhill. Sun were once one of the largest employers in the town and many popular journals were produced on their presses.

Acknowledgements

All the photographs in this book are in the local collection at Watford Central Library. I have tried to trace the photographers of the more recent pictures, but if I have inadvertently used any photographs without permission, I do apologize and hope that those who have been offended will contact me. Thanks to everyone at the Library for their patience while I was 'playing with those old photos' and to Kitty for being a good companion while I was typing. And finally, a very big thank-you to everyone who has the forethought and generosity to donate their photographs and postcards to local history collections everywhere!

Introduction

There is a seemingly endless interest in old photographs; perhaps not surprisingly, since they can document the changes in a community with greater immediacy than any other medium – and change and development are the very essence of local history, or indeed of any history. The changes may be quite local – perhaps the rise in importance of one shopping area while another sinks to a less significant commercial role, as we see in the see-sawing relationship between the High Street and Queen's Road. Or it may be the demolition of a group of buildings to make way for a car park or other new development, a fate which has befallen many a building in Watford. Sometimes the changes may reflect a national trend, as in the pedestrianization of Watford's High Street and provision of cycle routes in the late 1990s, which are attempts at putting into practice the idea of living in greater harmony with the environment. Part of the fascination of old photographs is in seeing what has changed and what remains, albeit in an altered state, and in recognizing – if we are honest – that today's innovations in planning, building design and lifestyle will be the antiquated curiosities of tomorrow.

Memory can play tricks on us and it is vital to try to date old photographs as accurately as possible; to this end the local historian draws on a variety of sources such as maps, directories, newspapers and census returns. Sometimes the photographer has been kind enough to scratch a precise date on the film, or one may be printed on a postcard, but often we need to play the detective and study evidence such as styles of hat, uniforms or car registration plates shown in the view.

Photographs are taken for a variety of reasons. They may be official, even technical, taken by planning departments, schools and other institutions largely for their own records or for public information. Some are commercial in origin; for example, there was mass production of postcards to satisfy the collecting boom in the early years of this century and many copies were published of scenes that might now be thought to be of only local significance. Other photographs were straightforward advertisements for a service or goods and often these would appear in the local street directories, such as Watford Kelly's and Peacock's, which had a wide distribution. Most amateur photographers' work is produced for purely personal satisfaction and the quality varies from the tilted 'snap' to the highly arranged scene; indeed, the small snapshot is sometimes the only example of an event or scene that exists in a local collection. The deliberately artistic or posed photograph does not have a place in a collection such as this – no pretty snow-sprinkled landscapes or dustbins glinting in the sunlight here! The emphasis in this book and in local public photographic collections is on the content, not the design. However, some of the very best work in the book, by Whitford Anderson and Frederick Downer, for example, is both informative *and* achieves photographic artistry. If the former had not recorded early buildings and churches across the whole of the county, and if Downer had not made the effort to attend every fire, flood or other notable event in Watford, we should be much poorer in our knowledge of the topography and excitements of the town's past.

A town is a living entity that changes as rapidly as the ideas of the people who live and work in it. Although fascinated by change, we are also rather frightened by it and many have a suspicion that things were better in former times. Of course some things were better, but anyone who thinks objectively about social conditions last century, or even up to the Second World War, must realize that a great number of things were not better at all. Deprivation is often poignantly depicted in photographs of schools, houses and other buildings, and in the faces of their inhabitants.

Looking at old photographs is immensely enjoyable, even if they cover an unfamiliar place, but they are also a very useful resource – for social, family and industrial historians and for children with their perennial school projects. Those who work with the elderly have also discovered that pictures of familiar places and faces from the past can help to stimulate mental activity in confused people. Finally, old photographs of their locality can be an excellent way of creating a common interest in a group of otherwise very disparate people – people of different ages, social backgrounds and ethnic groups. One thing they have in common is that they are all fascinated by the way *their* town has altered; I hope that past and present inhabitants of Watford will find plenty to interest them in this book.

The Great Storm of 27 July 1906 caught people at lunchtime, flooding cellars in Queen's Road and the High Street, including the basement of one of the town's electric light transformer stations. Lightning killed three sheep in Cassiobury Park and toppled a stone cross on the old chapel of Cassiobury House.

One
Leisure

The High Street decked out in June 1887 to celebrate Queen Victoria's Golden Jubilee. Several bands, including the Union Workhouse children's band, joined in the procession. The original lantern slide is by Frederick Downer, Watford's greatest photographer.

TO THE ELECTORS OF WATFORD.

The Park and the People.

Do not be DECEIVED by UNTRUE STATEMENTS.

IT IS UNTRUE	IT IS A FACT
That its purchase would mean a 4d. Rate.	That the purchase of 75 acres at £24,000 would only mean a 1½d. Rate which would gradually become less as the Rateable Value of the Town increased.
IT IS UNTRUE	IT IS A FACT
That Workmen would have to pay 6d. a week more Rent, because of the Park being bought.	That in 1903 the District Rate was 4/6; To-day it is 3/9; and as New Sources of Income are available, it should not be necessary to raise this Rate for the purchase.
IT IS UNTRUE	IT IS A FACT
That the People of LOWER HIGH STREET, CALLOW LAND, QUEEN'S WARD and HARWOODS ESTATE Do not Use the Park.	That the Thousands of People who use the Park come from every part of the Town.

FELLOW TOWNSMEN! If called upon to **VOTE** on this Question, think of your **WIVES** and **CHILDREN**, to whom this **PUBLIC PARK** would be a **BOON.**

Have a place to walk in that YOU can call YOUR OWN.

VOTE FOR ITS PURCHASE and save the Town from becoming a SECOND WEST HAM.

Published by Cassiobury Public Park Committee—JOSCELINE F. WATKINS, Chairman ; W. T. COLES, Vice-Chairman.   Printed by EDWARD VOSS, Loates Lane, Watford.

When the Earl of Essex sold part of Cassiobury Park in 1908 to Ashby and Brightman for development as a residential estate, they in turn offered some of this land to Watford Urban District Council as a public park. Feelings ran high in the town as one faction tried to persuade residents that the park would be a valuable amenity, while the other group concentrated on the possible burden on the rates. A vote among the townspeople in September 1908 resulted in a resounding 'No' to the public acquisition of the land, but a year later the Council bought 65 acres and made further purchases in later years.

At the coronation of George V and Queen Mary in June 1911 rejoicing took place all over Watford and the *West Herts Post* produced a celebratory issue in red type. Buildings were decorated and the front of the Conservative Club, seen here, 'stood out conspicuously smothered in Union Jacks and Stars and Stripes'. Lower down the social hierarchy the inmates of the workhouse were treated to chicken, salmon and a recital on the piano organ.

King Edward VII motored from Sandown Races to the Grove to stay with the Earl of Clarendon in July 1909. Although it was a private visit the King 'consented to a tribute of loyalty' from Watford inhabitants including a march of Boy Scouts from the High Street to the Grove. On Sunday he attended St Mary's church where admission was by ticket only.

Not a Coronation or a Jubilee this time, but a visit by the Prince of Wales to lay the foundation stone of the London Orphan Asylum on 15 July 1869. He arrived by train but was conveyed to the school site in the Earl of Essex's carriage. The children in the foreground are wearing the Old Free School dress.

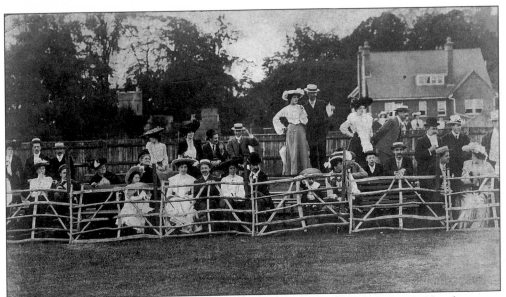

Part of Harwoods Farm was offered for the West Herts Sports Ground, but there was controversy over who should manage it: a company or a non-profit making trust? Intended for both cricket and football, the ground was rented very cheaply from the Earl of Essex and was acquired in perpetuity for the townspeople in 1922 by Benskins.

School sports held at the public open-air bathing place at Five Arches on the River Colne, probably between 1906 and 1914. The bathing place, maintained by the Corporation, had bathing boxes and mixed family bathing was allowed at certain times during the week. Unfortunately the health and fitness promoted by regular swimming was somewhat offset by the discovery in 1936 that the water was contaminated by sewage. One councillor complained that at times there were only ten or twelve inches of water at one end and three feet at the other, and she had been told of dead dogs and cats in the river. Not surprisingly the place was closed, though officials recognized that people would swim in the river anyway.

Two views of the opening of the Lord Hyde Memorial Camp, 3 July 1938. Lady Hyde (later the Countess of Clarendon) had been associated with the 1st Watford troop from the beginning of the movement in Watford. In 1936 Lord Clarendon gave three and a half acres of woodland in Lees Wood for a Scout camp to commemorate the death of their son George Lord Hyde. At the official opening the Bishop of St Albans conducted the dedication service and the address was given by Lord Hyde's uncle, the Deputy Chief Scout. He is in the centre of both photographs, while the Earl can be seen wearing an overcoat. The campsite is still in use.

An open-air thanksgiving service to celebrate King George V's Silver Jubilee was held in Cassiobury Park in May 1935. Amplifiers carried the sound to thousands of listeners. All elementary school children were given twelve penny vouchers to spend as they liked and 'a big proportion of this was invested in the amusements at Flanagan's Fair'.

Watford Grammar School cricket team, summer 1939. The team's finest hour was probably their match against the MCC in June 1934 when they achieved an honourable draw.

Rarely can there have been a more incongruous pair than the Mayor of Watford, Alderman Andrews, and the Carnival Queen enjoying – or enduring – a ride on the dodgems at the funfair in 1940.

Despite the war, people flocked to the Peace Memorial Hospital Saturday Fund carnival in August 1942. Here is the unopposed winner of the senior class in the bathing belle contest, with a group of self-conscious, sandalled young entrants.

About sixty decorated vehicles joined in a procession along Watford's main streets to mark the 1935 Jubilee. The fire brigade's new engine, called *Silver Jubilee*, put in its first public appearance and, in contrast, the old eighteenth-century parish engine was pulled along by a seventy-five-year-old former fireman.

Watford retained the EBA Associates challenge cup for the second year running when they beat the Civil Service in the finals in September 1949. The score was Watford 91, Civil Service 68.

The pond is frozen over and naturally the boys are playing as close to danger as possible! This photograph dates from some time in the 1950s; the impressive columns of the Odeon are on the left and the Chef Restaurant and Bakery can be seen on the site now occupied by Yates' wine bar.

WEMCO in Whippendell Road, the joint winner with Benskins of the prize for the best decorated industrial premises at the Coronation celebrations, June 1953.

The Mayor of Watford greets the Queen Mother in July 1965. The main purpose of her visit was to inspect the 1st Battalion of the Beds and Herts Regiment (TA), who paraded in Cassiobury Park.

The crowning of the May Queen at the Labour May Day procession in 1939 was a light note on an otherwise serious occasion. Many representatives of the Labour movement paraded into Callowland Recreation Ground, with an 'Aid for Spain' truck bringing up the rear. *The Red Flag* was played and banners proclaimed slogans such as 'Conscript wealth, not youth'.

The playground at Oxhey Park, looking towards Five Arches viaduct over the River Colne, *c.* 1950. The park was opened in 1919 on part of Wiggenhall Estate.

Morris dancers outside Moselle Gowns in the High Street. In the lower photograph a folk group entertains shoppers on the steps of Charter Place. Can anyone identify the occasion?

More entertainment in Charter Place. Opened in 1976 to commemorate the achievement of Borough status in 1922, Charter Place with its covered market, shops, multi-storey car park and YMCA hostel replaced Cawdells and the old market.

Unusual visitors to Watford, passing the now defunct Malden Hotel in Station Road after a march along Woodford Road. The picture probably dates from around 1950, but what was the occasion?

Enjoying the summer in Cassiobury Park, 1970s. These boys are demonstrating that well-known fact that the greatest fun is to be had when there is the greatest chance of grown-ups' disapproval!

The same group by the lock, contemplating their next move. Both of these photographs were taken by the late Harry Packman of Croxley.

Watford had dozens of street parties in early June 1977 to mark the Queen's Silver Jubilee. Unfortunately fine weather could not be guaranteed and many parties succumbed to cold winds and torrential rain and had to take to the shelter of school and church halls. So far the inclement weather has not reached the jelly, cakes and pop at this street party in Hamilton Road, South Oxhey.

An open-air art exhibition held in the late 1950s before the redevelopment at the crossroads. Walker's the cleaners and the Westminster Bank are just visible beneath the spreading chestnut tree.

The Carlton Cinema in Clarendon Road, seen here in 1974, finally closed its doors in July 1980. Originally opened as the Super Cinema in a converted skating rink, it became the Carlton in 1930 after extensive refurbishment. Palace theatregoers today who have a meal in the Green Room restaurant are on the site of the former cinema.

Some of these revellers at the Watford Junior Library Halloween party in October 1977 may now be bringing their own children to the regular story-time sessions.

Two
Shops and Trade

The entrance to Red Lion Yard in 1903. The yard, named after the public house, cut though to Beechen Grove from the Market Place. Pearkes' Stores and Tea Dealers were next to the tobacconists but the area was partially burnt and pulled down in 1918.

Joseph Dorrofield opened his stationery shop in Queen's Road in the late 1880s and in 1900 it became the property of G.T. Dukes. The original of this fine photograph came from Miss Dukes and has 'G.T. Dukes 1904' pencilled on the back. So is this Mr Dukes before the shop's name changed, or is this Mr Dorrofield himself?

An advertisement from Peacock's directory, 1894. Dorrofield was obviously proud of his former connection with the famous Dickinson company; in 1881 he was an envelope maker at Apsley Mill. All his advertisements insisted on the 'manufacturing' of stationery, not just the supply of ready-made goods.

Cattle standing outside Mortimer's the butcher in the High Street, c. 1910. The original postcard was found in an old sideboard in an antique shop in Australia, with a note on the back: 'This town is about 8 miles from Hendon and it is a fairly busy town.' The purchaser of the sideboard sent the card to Watford Library.

The Bucks and Oxon Bank in the High Street, shortly before 1900. It was absorbed by Lloyds Bank in around 1904. Next door was Bruton's drapers and funeral furnishers.

Looking north up the nearly deserted High Street where the Clements flag is flying. When the flyover was built the far wing of Clements was demolished. Sainsburys remained next door until around 1972 when it moved to Queen's Road. Both shops celebrated their centenary in Watford in 1998.

Number 97 High Street in 1903, photographed by A. Whitford Anderson, architect and historian, who practised in Watford from 1893. His photographs of Hertfordshire churches and other structures form a superb record of demolished and altered buildings. Frederick Downer, the photographer, lived in this house from 1882 to 1886 and subsequently David Downer ran a stationery business here.

In contrast to the picture opposite, Clements here is seething with be-hatted bargain hunters. Postmarked 1907, the card bears the message 'This is Clements shilling sale. Note Ted on bike; I don't think he went to the sale.'

Clem Childs' hairdressing shop in St Albans Road. The range of goods and services was diverse, and some wag has inscribed on the photograph 'There's a hairdresser in Watford named Childs; He has shaved some thousands of Dials.'

An advertisement from Peacock's
directory of 1906. The firm was still
operating in 1986.

Fred Oatley, tailor, on the New Road
corner of the High Street, *c.* 1910. He
has a striking window display with a
satirical touch.

Jaeger garments, made of pure wool, were central to the 'rational dress' movement which started in the 1880s. Dr Jaeger's sanitary woollen combinations may have sold well at Waite's outfitters, but the market in Watford for air-chamber helmets was probably limited! This advertisement appeared in 1915.

The view down the High Street in 1921 with the Pru and Clements on the left and the turning to Upton Road on the right. The shady foreground obscures the entrance to Watford Council offices.

Three High Street shops, *c.* 1927. Christmas and Co. adapted with the times – they evolved from a coachbuilders to a garage.

The Clarendon Road corner of the High Street, *c.* 1932. The official guide commented wordily, 'With so many fine shops in the town, one secures all of the advantages of the larger choice which is generally claimed as exclusive to London, without the disadvantages of the expenditure of money and energy attendant upon a journey to Town.'

Dudley's Corner in the High Street, just south of Clarendon Road. Apart from the gown shop itself there were confectioners, fruiterers, an optician and, in Dudley's Chambers on the first floor, the Loosley Registry Office for servants, which survived until the Second World War. Note the Peace notice on the stump of the last lime tree, after which the former Lime Tree Hotel was named.

Wings for Victory Week in May 1943 opened with the release of pigeons outside the Town Hall. The library had an exhibition of posters and model planes by local schoolchildren, and Clements' windows displayed Mosquito aircraft among the hats.

P. BUCK'S

Exceptional Suite of Rooms

Suitable for Private Dances, Banquets, Wedding Receptions, Concerts, etc.
52 HIGH STREET, WATFORD

In addition to their restaurant and ballroom, advertised here in 1933, Buck's provided 'plain and fancy bread, dinner rolls and bride cakes', and hired out cutlery, marquees and bazaar fittings. They moved to Exchange Road in the early 1960s but survived only a few years.

The High Street no longer has the same interesting variety of shops adjacent to one another: a confectioner, a hosier, a pork butcher, a dental repairer, a hairdresser, a dry cleaner and a draper. This view dates from 1952.

The High Street, c. 1955. The 1956 Official Guide states that 'although the main shopping thoroughfares – High Street, Queens Road, Market Street and St Albans Road – tend to become congested at busy times, this only seems to add to the enjoyment, for many revel in the experience of being in a crowd of excited shoppers.' The Harlequin Centre has now attracted most of these happy spenders away from the older shopping areas.

W.J. Elliott's on the Upton Road corner of the High Street sold pianos, music, records, radios and televisions. In the 1890s the original shop in Queen's Road boasted the largest stock of pianos in the county as well as a circulating music library for a membership fee of a guinea a year. The buildings shown here were demolished in 1957.

Dumbleton's the butchers in the Lower High Street, c. 1964. The passing car contrasts with this old timber-framed building that was demolished to make way for 'modern' Watford.

Three
Pubs and Breweries

Benskins Watford Brewery with the 'Pennant' flying. The origin of this trademark was that Thomas Benskin, an enthusiastic yachtsman, told his daughter he wanted a simple design, 'a flag flying would be a good thing.' She copied the flag from her own brooch and this remained their insignia. The offices in the foreground, formerly the Benskin residence, now house Watford Museum.

The delivery yard at Sedgwick's Brewery. The Sedgwick family acquired an existing brewery on the east side of the Lower High Street in the 1860s and had it rebuilt some ten years later. In 1924 the brewery was taken over by Benskins, whose premises were on the opposite side of the road.

The Hit or Miss pub and the Anchor beerhouse in the Lower High Street in 1893. The former was rebuilt in 1898 and was finally demolished in the mid 1990s as part of the 'improved' road system.

The Railway Tavern in 1903, photographed by Whitford Anderson who noted that this group of buildings was dated 1714. He also took the upper photograph.

The Compasses on the corner of Market Street, in 1898. Its famous window can be seen on the left; when the pub was rebuilt in the 1920s the window was preserved on the ground floor and is still intact. To the north is the Green Man – Watford has never been short of places to have a drink!

Sedgwick's Brewery volunteer fire brigade. It had its own steam fire engine and was under the control of Captain Sedgwick himself. An electric call system connected it to the central station of the Watford fire brigade in the High Street.

A view of the back of the Red Lion public house in 1903, seen from the cobbled courtyard that cut though from the High Street to Beechen Grove. There were over thirty houses in Red Lion Yard.

An early Edwardian view of the Rose and Crown. By the mid-nineteenth century it offered large stables, rooms to hire to local societies for meetings and The Meadow at the back which was used for auctions and cattle sales.

A busy scene as farmers and traders survey the livestock at the open-air market in the High Street. The market remained here until 1928. The date of this photograph is revealed by the poster in the background – 'Your country needs You'.

The personnel of Benskins cooperage in 1932. Virtually all the work was done by hand; no nails were used, only heat and pressure to bend the oak staves into the required shape. A good cask was expected to last over twenty years.

A cartoon from the Benskins house journal in 1932. Perhaps the artist was inspired by the frequent flooding of the Lower High Street!

How tastes change! Benskins were so proud of their new Compasses public house (above) in 1932, but today most people would probably prefer the character of the old building (below). Compare the photograph on p. 42 when the pub was still a Sedgwick house.

Another page from Benskin's house journal in 1932 showing the recently renovated Compasses in 'thirties Tudor' décor. Later it was renamed the Joseph Benskin, and later still its premises were used as a shoe shop and more recently by Moss Bros, tailors.

A view of Cassio Hamlet in 1934 from the Central Library. The Horns is opposite with the public baths in the background.

One of the few pictures of the Dog, Cassio Hamlet. The picture was taken in the mid-1930s when the Hempstead Road was being widened. The pub was demolished in 1970.

Brewers have traditionally employed heavy horses to draw their drays, and a few still do – they can be more economical than motor power for short journeys. These are two of Benskins Clydesdales in 1939.

The Halfway House at Cassio Bridge in 1956, with the railway line to Croxley in the background.

The building next to the tool hire shop in Lower High Street was formerly the Fox beerhouse, which was demolished in 1956 after the lease ended the same year. The alleyway at the side led through to Watford Field Road.

The Swan to the south of Fox Alley, in 1957. At this date the proprietor also ran the Swan Judo School on the premises.

A hairdressing salon now occupies the premises of the Three Crowns, seen here in 1958. Next door but one was – and still is – the One Crown public house. The Three Crowns was once called The Crown, but in 1750 the name changed to avoid confusion with the new One Crown.

'Strong drink preys on man and spreads its dark wings over many a happy household' – a temperance tract of 1878 on the sign of the Spread Eagle. This mid-eighteenth-century building with many later alterations was provisionally 'listed' in 1948 but was demolished ten years later.

The former Jolly Farmers on the corner of St Albans Road and West Street closed in 1958. For most of this century it was run by the Mendham family.

The Kings Arms was once a handsome building, converted from the entrance lodge to Watford Place. The carriage drive later became King Street. It was considered for 'listing' in 1948. This photograph was taken in 1961 shortly before demolition to make way for Woolworths.

The Railway Arms in St Albans Road was pulled down in 1961 when the railway bridge was widened. The original Watford station stood nearly opposite and the station house is now a garage.

The Clarendon Hotel in need of restoration, seen from Station Approach. It opened in 1862 and closed in 1976, and later became the head offices of Benskin's. Now (1998) it is the Flag and Firkin.

The One Crown in 1977. This listed building dates from the sixteenth century, though its use as an inn did not begin until 1750.

The Victoria public house at the junction of Queen's Road and Loates Lane in 1978. Known as the Tantivy in 1873 it changed its name to the Victoria within a year, but from 1980 it reverted to the Tantivy – and recently has come round once again to Victoria! No wonder local historians get confused. And how strange that there should be horse riders in such an urban site; are they looking for the Tantivy stagecoach?

Four
A Transport Miscellany

Four modes of transport: Bushey Arches in the late 1920s, showing cars, horse-drawn vehicles, a bicycle and a sign advertising frequent electric trains to London 'and all parts'.

A working boat on the Grand Union Canal, photographed by John Cullen between 1904 and 1914.

Bushey Hall Road during the flood on 16 June 1903. 'The overflow of the river completely inundated the pathway along the bank from the direction of the Wheatsheaf Inn, and a large water-covered tract of land, resembling a natural lake, extended from Hamper Mill.' The *Watford Observer* wrote of 'imprisoned householders' and of a postman who delivered letters to upper windows with a fishing net. The Council provided all kinds of vehicles to convey people to and from Bushey.

THE £10,000 AEROPLANE FLIGHT FROM LONDON TO MANCHESTER

The Daily Mail offered a £10,000 prize to the winner of a London to Manchester flight. Aviator Grahame White passed over Watford at 5.35 in the morning and 'this was the first time a flying machine had been seen in the Watford district.' The Englishman was beaten by Louis Paulham but 'few will forget the jolly hand waves as we stood on Callow Land Bridge early on Saturday morning.'

THE GREAT STORM and BLIZZARD. Tuesday, March 28th, 1916
Motor Car cut in two by a falling tree in Grove Mill Lane. The Driver and two lady occupants escaped as the tree was falling.

The Great Storm of 28 March 1916 was complicated by heavy drifting snow. Market stalls blew over, shop windows blew in, flood waters rose in the Lower High Street and hundreds of trees fell across roads, telegraph wires and tram lines. Foraging parties took advantage of a ready supply of firewood!

Buses outside the Junction station between 1913 and 1915. The ladies are eager to display their hats to full advantage on the upper deck.

Cassio Bridge in 1922 when a temporary bridge was built. Presumably the policeman, looking slightly surreal, is surveying its safety.

An advertisement from Peacock's directory of 1929.

LEWIS' COACHES

Sole Booking & Enquiry Office: **25, MARKET ST., WATFORD**

26 & 32 SEATERS *for* **PRIVATE HIRE**

Hail, Rain, or Shine—Comfort all the time.

For Daily Trips, Coastal and other Tours during Summer Season, see Boards at LEWIS' GARAGE, 25, Market Street.

The Coaches are the latest All-Weather models, fitted with pneumatic tyres. They offer you a first-rate service, for they give you comfort and absolute safety, combined with all-round efficiency and reliability SECOND-TO-NONE.

LEWIS' OMNIBUSES also operate a regular daily service between Watford and Rickmansworth, and also between WATFORD and WINDSOR, via Chorley Wood, Chenies, The Chalfonts, Gerrards Cross, Fulmer, Wexham and Slough. Cheap Return Tickets are available on both routes.

The telephone is always at your service, why not telephone your enquiries. Our number is **WATFORD 488.**

*"TO TRAVEL IN COMFORT. WITHOUT ANY FUSS.
BE SURE YOU RIDE ON A LEWIS BUS,
OR. IF BEAUTY SPOTS YOU WOULD APPROACH.
ALWAYS RIDE ON A LEWIS COACH."*

Wiggenhall Bridge over the Colne, in March 1925. This was still a rural scene with a view across Watford Fields towards the breweries.

One of Benskins lorries used for deliveries in London in 1931, driven by W. Bone.

This Scammell street washer demonstrated in Watford in 1936 could be adapted for two other uses: as a decontaminator of poison gas, or as a fire-fighting unit.

The High Street in April 1939, with a chaotic mix of driven and parked cars, buses, delivery vans and bicycles. Wartime petrol rationing would soon restrict the traffic.

It may look fun, but floods in spring 1947 caused such hardship that the Mayor opened a relief fund. The Highway Superintendent said that the snow and gales made St Albans Road and Market Street look like 'miniature Himalayas'.

Watford Junction in 1977 before the mid-1980s alterations that completely rebuilt the station entrance, with extensive office space above.

Scammell Motors, which moved to Tolpits Lane in 1922, were one of Watford's most important companies. They produced vehicles for a variety of uses including military, haulage and oilfield construction. This is one of their 'Contractor' range, introduced in 1964.

Five

Change and
Development

ATFORD FROM THE PARISH CHURCH TOWER.

DOWNER.
COPYRIGHT

An early semi-aerial view by Frederick Downer of the High Street looking towards Beechen Grove, c. 1907.

Derby Road, *c.* 1907, with Watford Grammar School, now Central Primary, in the foreground and the Strict Baptist tabernacle behind it. Queen's Road Wesleyan church is in the background.

The footpath to Albert Road in June 1928. The following April the Plaza cinema opened on land which had formerly been the grounds of a house called Elmcote and it remained, later renamed the Odeon, until 1963.

A hospital for £50,000? The Peace Memorial Hospital appeal actually raised £90,000. The statutes governing the hospital stated that the object was to provide treatment, advice and medicines to the sick within the borough and surrounding area. It specifically excluded heavily pregnant women, epileptics, incurables, the insane and those with infectious diseases, all of whom were catered for in other institutions.

Woodland Drive, which followed the course of the Green Drive from Little Cassiobury, was developed in 1927. At first the houses did not have numbers, only names such as Lulworth, The Nook and Meanwhile.

Monmouth House photographed by Whitford Anderson in 1898. An early seventeenth-century building, it had already been greatly changed and its alteration in 1929 into shops transformed it completely.

The crossroads and pond in May 1935. The Elms stands on what is now the Town Hall site. The sharp-sighted may spot the AA box and man in the road directing the non-existent traffic.

A closer view of the crossroads before the 1936 'improvements' when a roundabout was constructed to deal with the increasing traffic. Little Nascot, by now a maternity clinic, is being partially demolished on the left, while sites for shops are up for sale at the top of the Parade.

Another site for shop development: the Cassiobury Drive roundabout in the late 1950s.

Kimpton Place on the post-war Garston Park housing estate. The borough in its 1947 housing exhibition brochure recognized that 'the housing problem is the most serious social and moral problem we have'.

The Harebreaks was the first major council housing estate, built in 1920 and modernized in the 1970s. In 1946-47, during the post-war housing crisis, nearly forty Universal Asbestos temporary houses were added to the estate.

Building the Town Hall in summer 1938, to replace the Council Offices in Upton Road. It was built to a design by Cowles-Voysey, following an architectural competition; public reaction was not entirely favourable.

The pond and Parade in 1954 with the traffic going in all directions. No wonder so much municipal effort has gone into reorganizing the traffic in the town!

The southern end of St Albans Road, *c.* 1960. The shops on the left were later demolished to make way for the Beechen Grove ring road.

The last days of Meeting Alley, *c.* 1961. The road cut through from the High Street to Beechen Grove where the Baptist church can be seen.

The bridle path from the Junction station towards St Albans Road in 1961. The pedestrian tunnel was built the following year.

Rebuilding the Junction station, February 1985. A spokesman for British Rail emphasized that it was going to be 'a very modern place indeed with a new travel centre with up-to-the-minute aids.' Further modernization, including the installation of automatic gates, occurred in 1998.

The central area Highway Proposals were originally presented in 1963, leading to a long period of public consultation and a Public Inquiry. They were finally adopted in 1968 and were divided into eight phases that took some ten years to complete. This shows part of phase 3, the construction of the St Albans Road underpass in 1972.

Six
Gone Forever!

Monmouth House still stands, though much modified, but the stark elegance of the drawing room with its exposed beams and highly polished floor reflects an age that is past.

Hyde Lodge in Clarendon Road, 1900; photograph by William Coles. The inscription reads 'Residence of Mr Hollingsworth, a farmer. Built in 1880.' He was probably the Charles Hollingsworth who had run Nether Wylde Farm near Bricket Wood.

A later view of Hyde Lodge, shortly after it was vacated by the postal sorting office in 1964. It was situated near the station next to the Trade Union and Labour Club.

Stanley Camp, solicitor and one-time chairman of the Library Committee, outside Wisteria House in the High Street, just south of Water Lane. He lived and ran his practice here and died here in 1900.

Swiss Cottage in Cassiobury Park, described by Britton in 1837 as being 'on the banks of the River Gade, intended for a family, and also for the accommodation of parties during the summer, to take refreshment.' The cottages were lived in by estate workers.

Dr Tibble's Vi-Cocoa works were built in 1899 on a site by the St Albans branch line close to Windsor Road. The product was advertised as 'favoured by the homes and hospitals of Great Britain' and as being 'of undoubted purity and strength.'

The largest fire that Watford has known broke out on Saturday 7 February 1903 in the Vi-Cocoa works. The hooter was blown and the fire brigades from Watford, Bushey, Sedgwick's Brewery and Northwood arrived to find a blazing furnace. It was impossible to save the factory. Some chocolate compound melted onto the railway sidings and caked the sleepers and hundreds of tons of cocoa beans were ruined. Six hunred people were made unemployed during the rebuilding of the factory.

'Old House in Water Lane' photographed by Whitford Anderson in 1893. He subsequently noted that the chimney had gone by April 1908 and the whole house was demolished in 1912.

The Literary Institute in Carey Place, founded in 1854, served as the town's library and adult education institute until the Public Library Act of 1874. The 1858 library catalogue included works by Scott, Dickens and the Brontës as well as the *Illustrated London News*.

House in Church Street showing a decorative, possibly Tudor, bargeboard – the inclined wooden board beneath the gable, covering the rafters. It was later removed to the museum in the Public Library.

Watford House stood in the High Street near the present Clarendon Road. The house was lived in by Dr Brett, Medical Officer of Health and social benefactor of Watford; it had formerly been occupied by Robert Clutterbuck, the Hertfordshire historian.

The last days of the Elms, September 1937. This fine early eighteenth-century house was knocked down to make way for the Town Hall. When the town received its charter in 1922 the Elms itself was considered as future Council Chambers and offices.

One of the handsome houses in Clarendon Road. Number 51, for many years a doctor's surgery and later an insurance office, was demolished in 1959.

Beechen Grove Baptist Sunday school in 1963, later demolished to make way for road changes. Between the school in Meeting Alley and the car park was the graveyard where many significant members of the early Baptist community were buried.

'Scared to the memory of Mrs Eliza Harding, died 1835. Also Rebecca Harding, died 1826. Mothers of the Church.' A Local Act of Parliament in 1963 authorized the use of the burial ground for other purposes, and the remains were re-interred at Vicarage Road.

Gartlet School moved from Loates Lane to Clarendon Road in 1897 and under a succession of strong-minded headmistresses, gave a good education to girls for the next sixty years. The school moved to Nascot Wood Road in 1949 to a private house with extensive grounds; these premises are now occupied by the Watford School of Music.

'O strong is the law at school that binds us
To all that is right and true;
That we in our lives may be fair and just
In whatever we have to do.'
(From the Gartlet School song)

GARTLET SCHOOL, WATFORD.

In 1613 Dame Mary Morrison of Cassiobury gave money for the maintenance of four poor widows. These almshouses in Vicarage Road were rebuilt in 1824 in what Pevsner dismissively called 'uninteresting neo-Gothic style'. Uninteresting or not, they fell victim to town centre improvements.

People using the short cut from Station Road to Shady Lane may wonder at the name Verulam Passage. Here the Verulam Hotel, first mentioned in a directory of 1859, is being demolished in 1958.

Albert Street, once known as Chater's Yard, ran parallel to Queen's Road off the High Street. The houses seen here were pulled down in the early 1960s and now the whole area lies beneath the Harlequin Centre.

Brookmans Garage opened in 1921 at the southern end of St Albans Road. It was acquired by Tucker Brothers in the early 1950s and closed in 1968/69.

Carey Place, which connected the High Street with Derby Road, was named after Jonathan Carey, a plasterer, who developed the yard in the mid-nineteenth century. The photograph records the demolition of part of the street in 1961/62.

The British Moulded Hose Factory in Sandown Road employed 2,000 people in the 1940s, but by the early 1970s the workforce had been reduced to a tenth of this. The firm moved to Lancashire in 1977 and the manufacturing plant was demolished. It had suffered a massive fire in 1961, by coincidence on the site of the Vi-Cocoa works fire nearly sixty years before.

Seven

Wartime Watford

Troops from the 42nd (Hertfordshire) Company, Imperial Yeomanry mobilizing in Watford in 1900. Each man had to provide himself with 'Ankle boots, brown, 2 pairs. Canvas shoes, 1 pair. Braces or belt. Brushes, hair, 1. Brushes, cloth, 1. Table fork. Table spoon. Drawers, 2 pairs. Khaki flannel shirts, 2. Worsted socks, 3 pairs. Bootlaces, brown, 3 pairs. Razor. Set of saddlery.'

First World War ammunition works, sited on the estate near Balmoral Road. A potentially horrendous fire in February 1917 was dealt with by the Watford fire brigade and resulted in five medals awarded for gallantry.

Members of the London Scottish Regiment near the pond. They were the first of the territorial regiments to go to France in September 1914, having trained for a month at Leavesden. On their departure, several shops reported 'great trade, people buying tobacco etc. to give to the men.'

An air-raid siren used during the Second World War, sited at the corner of Bushey Mill Lane and Tudor Avenue. The photograph was taken in November 1938.

The Mayor, Cllr Horwood, drinking to the success of Watford's Milk Week in 1938; in his speech he referred to the craze for milk bars of which more than 1,200 had opened all over the country. Milk shortages followed during the war and products like Allenbury's Diet ('more delicious, more nourishing and more easily digested than plain milk') were advertised regularly in the *Watford Observer*.

10,000 spectators watched a National Service recruiting procession and display in Cassiobury Park in May 1939. It included a mock air attack by three RAF aeroplanes and the burning of a building specially constructed for the event. The 'casualties', the Boy Scouts in the photograph, were ferried to a dressing station and hospital.

The ARP Rescue and Demolition Unit also took part in the aftermath of the mock attack, using the lorry of Brightman's the builders. They are pausing outside Beechen Grove church where the prayer notice seems somehow incongruous.

Watford prepared for emergencies during the first week of September 1939, sand-bagging the windows of the Peace Memorial Hospital, Shrodell's and the King Street Maternity Home. Here bags are being prepared and gathered in the car park.

Women volunteers filling mattresses with straw at the Peace. The accommodation was increased and all but the most seriously ill patients were sent home as the hospital was put on war-time alert.

New motoring regulations at the outbreak of war required bumpers to be painted white because of the blackout. Here the Revd Ireson of St James's church adds two extra white spots at the rear.

Children evacuated from London County Council schools arrived in Watford the day before war was declared. Officials are trying to cheer up this group gathered in the Watford Labour Club before dispersal to Aldenham, Radlett and Abbots Langley.

Further movements of children took place throughout September 1939. Some were dispersed in Hertfordshire and others were 'entrained' at the Junction to go further afield.

Another group of evacuated children in September 1939. Does any one recognize these smiling youngsters?

Early Civil Defence Volunteers in November 1939. They are wearing CD badges but have no uniforms as yet, except for those who are St John Ambulance or Red Cross workers.

It may look like an illustration for *Cold Comfort Farm*, but this man is delivering food scraps from householders for the Corporation's herd of pedigree pigs at Holywell Farm. For this extra work dustmen received a shilling for each hundredweight collected and surplus food was sold off to local farmers.

Scouts took part in the salvage drive of July 1940, but the local paper reported that people were stealing from the old iron dumps.

The salvage drive continued. In contrast to the Scouts' mountain of bicycles and railings, the Guides have a collection of more domestic items.

Wartime restrictions prevented papers from reporting the exact site where bomb damage occurred. The local paper said of one high explosive bomb, now known to have fallen on Eastlea Avenue, that it fell 'upon a new housing estate in the Home Counties. It demolished a house and killed four, including two girls.'

County Window Cleaning, the prize winners in the May carnival, probably 1940.

Children seated on a gun outside the Town Hall in War Weapons Week, April-May 1941. This was the first of the 'big weeks' to encourage National Savings; Watford and surrounding areas saved over £1,200,000.

A contemporary account stated that 'an Anderson shelter withstood blows when a bomb fell in a back garden and damaged several houses in a town in the Home Counties last week.' This almost certainly referred to Norfolk Avenue, hit in January 1941.

The first call-up order for women, for the over 21s, was issued in April 1941. Here Watford women are registering at the Employment Exchange.

It may have been wartime but there were other preoccupations on the domestic front, as these two 1940 advertisements show. The Silverdale Laundry cordially invited any visitor to the premises to see for herself (note the assumption!) the care that was given to articles entrusted to them.

HEALTH FIRST

It's healthier to keep the washing out of the home. Why not avoid chills and fatigue by using the Silverdale Services?

Call at one of our depots or 'phone for our van to collect a trial bundle. Attractive Secondary Service . . . . .

For Health's Sake Use the Laundry

2 EXCELLENT SERVICES

Fully Finished Service

For high-class work, beautifully laundered at reasonable charges.

Silversave Service

A complete household service for more moderate incomes.

SILVERDALE LAUNDRY, Ltd.

200, Rickmansworth Road, WATFORD.

Telephone: Watford 3305-6

DEPOTS : 272, St. Alban's Road, Watford.
15, Station Parade, Northwood.

Learning to be a satisfied customer of
THE
WATFORD STEAM LAUNDRY
LIMITED
SYDNEY ROAD, WATFORD   *Telephone* 4407

A rival company boasted of similar exceptional care for the laundry of discriminating customers.

The Hertfordshire Home Guard camped at Russells over the August Bank Holiday in 1941. The Lord Lieutenant and HQ staff inspected the camp and took lunch in the officers' mess. This is probably not what the cooks in the photograph are preparing!

WVS workers in March 1943 are serving tea outside the Town Hall. The van was supplied by the British War Relief Society and the Red Cross in America and has a Wyoming plaque on the side.

Eight
Some Watford Personalities

A group of unknown labourers clearing the bed of the River Colne, watched by uniformed men on the right. This picture could date from the General Strike of 1926, when soldiers were sometimes brought in to accompany and protect strike-breaking workers.

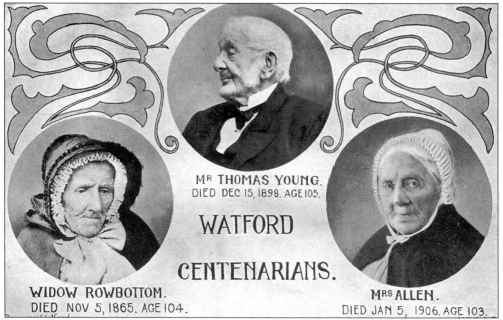

MR THOMAS YOUNG.
DIED DEC 15, 1898. AGE 105.

WATFORD

CENTENARIANS.

WIDOW ROWBOTTOM.
DIED NOV 5, 1865. AGE 104.

MRS ALLEN.
DIED JAN 5, 1906. AGE 103.

Evidence from the Census suggests the Thomas Young, a draper, died when he was a mere ninety-seven! Fanny Allen, an inmate of the Watford Union infirmary, had chosen high tea for her friends on the ward on her recent birthday and was 'very cheerful and lively at Xmas, and entered into the festivities of the Workhouse'. Of the widow we know nothing.

A studio portrait of the Chater brothers, c. 1870. E.M. Chater, left, entered his father's High Street chemist business in about 1850, but his lasting fame came from his educational work. Chater Schools were named after him. He was also connected with the public library management, chairing the University Extension Society. Prominent, like his father, in the Beechen Grove Baptist church, he died in 1909.

Professor John Attfield in his garden at Ashlands, Langley Road. When he retired from his post at the Pharmaceutical Society in 1897, a testimonial signed by hundreds of past students from the UK and abroad was given and a portrait made by Herkomer the artist, whose daughter Attfield later married. One of Attfield's past chemistry students was Watford photographer William Coles.

When Watford Public Library opened in October 1874 there was no money to appoint a permanent librarian, so for nine years the administration was carried out voluntarily. The first full-time librarian stayed only two years and was succeeded in August 1885 by John Woolman, seen here. Under his guidance the library expanded, borrowing fees were abolished and the educational work flourished.

George Bolton took over from Woolman in 1919 and remained librarian for over thirty years. He oversaw the move from the Queen's Road building to the library's present site and played a prominent part in wartime activities as Controller of No. 17 Group Royal Observer Corps Centre.

Bolton was enthusiastic about local history, particularly regarding the need to maintain a photographic collection showing changes in the town. We owe a great deal to him.

Watford Football Club with Alderman Thorpe during the 1906/07 season, by the stadium at the West Herts Ground in Cassio Road. The club had been champions of the United League the previous season and are proudly displaying the cup.

The Revd Fairlie Clarke, vicar of St Andrew's from 1915 to 1930, with his wife and daughter. The church opened in 1857 to serve the inhabitants of Watford 'New Town', the area near the Junction station to the west of St Albans Road.

The Salvation Army songsters and cadet corps, *c.* 1933. Major and Mrs Thornet are in the front row and their daughter, with plaits, is in the middle row. The background is probably the Citadel in St Mary's Road.

Ted Ray – not to be confused with the comedian of the same name – retired after twenty-nine years as a professional at Oxhey Golf Club, in May 1940.

Louis Burleigh Bruhl inspecting the Watford Art Society exhibition in the Public Library. He was born in Baghdad, educated in Vienna and trained as a doctor, but forsook medicine for art. An enthusiastic teacher of art, he was known particularly for his landscapes. He died in 1942 and was buried in Vicarage Road.

Cartoon depicting George Longley, draper and prominent citizen, who became a target for the Coronation Riots in 1902. He chaired the UDC twice, and he said he 'found keener antagonism than most candidates' because he was 'an enemy of the licensing trade'. He was a member of Watford Burial Board and a great economist – hence this drawing! He died in 1937.

Jack Butcher, who died in 1913, was for many years kennel man to the Old Berkley Hunt which was active in Buckinghamshire and Hertfordshire. From 1862 the hounds were kept at Chorley Wood and the hunt sometimes met at the Elms in Watford. On one occasion the Earl of Essex took the Hunt to court for operating in Cassiobury Park.

Nine
Public Services

The Victoria Cottage Hospital, Vicarage Road, from a lantern slide by Frederick Downer. It was built in 1885 and the Peace Memorial Hospital was intended to replace it. In fact the building remained.

Leavesden Asylum opened in October 1870 for the Metropolitan Asylum Board intended for 'harmless imbeciles' from London. It was a self-contained institution with its own chapel and workshops; within a year there were over 2,000 inmates. The hospital finally closed in 1995.

The Nurses' Home in Alexandra Road was opened by the Duchess of Gloucester in June 1940 and this photograph was probably taken shortly afterwards. It was intended for general midwifery and nursing staff, not those employed in hospitals. 'Purses' were given by many individuals and groups, including the Alexandra Infants' School, the Girl Guides and Scammell Lorries.

A fine selection of hats at the laying of the foundation stone of the District Nurses' Home in October 1939.

Probationer nurses receiving their preliminary training in the lecture hall in at Shrodells in December 1942.

The Earl of Clarendon unveiling the statue outside the Peace Memorial Hospital on 18 July 1928. The three figures in the statue by Mary Pownall Bromet represented mourning, those who

won through 'still whole in body and mind' and the wounded. The statue is now by the Town Hall.

WHAT IT MUST COME TO.

A cartoon from around 1873, showing the Revd Newton Price driving the Free Library chariot and capsizing the Literary Institute. There were many people opposed to the building of a public library in Watford; they considered that the old Literary Institute was adequate, but the Revd Newton Price of Oxhey was a leading force in the pro-library group.

From Peacock's Watford directory of 1894.

WATFORD

PUBLIC LIBRARY

COLLEGE OF

SCIENCE, ART, MUSIC, & LITERATURE.

School of Science, Art, & Literature.

GROUP I.—ART COURSES.—Head Master : MR. GEO. A. WOOD (Certificated Highest Grade by the Department of Science and Art in Groups I., II., III., and VI.), late Lecturer on Anatomy and Figure Drawing in the National Art Training School. Fees—Day Students, £1 10s. a Term ; Evening Students, 12s. 6d. and 2s. 6d. Embroidery and Needlework (Instructor, Miss Emily Yaxley) and Woodcarving (Instructor, Mr. W. Högh). Day Students, 12s. 6d. each subject ; Evening Students, 7s. 6d. and 2s. 6d. each subject.

GROUP II.—SCIENCE COURSES.—Courses in Geometry, Machine Construction, Building Construction, Carpentry and Joinery, Sanitary Work, Mathematics, Theoretical Mechanics, Applied Mechanics, Botany, Agriculture and Horticulture, and Hygiene. Fee—21s. each complete course ; Industrial Students, 5s.

GROUP III.—COMMERCIAL COURSES.—Courses in Arithmetic and Mensuration, Book-keeping, Commercial English, French, and Shorthand. Fees as in Group II.

UNIVERSITY EXTENSION COURSES in Literature and Science. Fee—one guinea for the two courses or 12s. 6d. each course.

School of Music.

Separate instruction in Singing, from 35s. to 60s. ; in Piano, from 15s. to 52s. 6d. ; in Violin, from 25s. to 55s. a Term. Instructors : Mr. C. MARSHALL (Head Master), Messrs. ARNOLD, COX, CUMMINGS, CUNLIFFE, FORRESTER, GREEN, HOPKINS, KUMMER, RAIMO, and WRIGHT, and Miss GRINDLEY. Junior Instructors : Miss ETHERIDGE and Mr. C. R. GIRARDOT.

For Prospectus and Particulars apply to the Secretary, JOHN WOOLMAN, Public Library, Watford.

The borough's mobile library service being plugged into its electricity supply. The cab and trailer were both made locally by Scammell.

ALDERTONS CIRCULATING LIBRARY
$1\frac{1}{2}$ Per Volume Only
Why Pay More.

**May we call each week on you, Over 3,000
Volumes to choose from. Absolutely
Modern Reading, Fiction, Drama, Romance,
Thrillers, Western, All the best authors.
Would you like your library books FREE?**
   Why of course you would,
   **Well. we now propose to ask you to
study our following proposition carefully.**

*W*e have a large Drapery and Furnishing department, from which
we can supply you with anything for the house home or person.
Now, we are in the happy position of being able to obtain an
unlimited number of books, through our various trade conne—
ctions, and after careful consideration, we can supply you
entirely free of charge our library volumes each week.
By opening an account with us to the value of sixpence, you
are entitled to two volumes without charge and you of course
get credited with Sixpence on account.
Likewise, by paying in One Shilling weekly, you are supplied
with four volumes, with One Shilling credited to your account
and we exchange your books in the usual way each week,
You may place an order any time you wish with us, and
you do not have to wait an irritating period before you obtain
your goods. An account of Fifteen Shillings is payable at Six—
pence per week, two books included, Thirty Shillings, at One
Shilling per week, four books included, For larger amounts,
you will find we shall be very pleased to make most reasonable
terms. Dresses, Suits, Casements, Lino, Rugs, Furniture, Cycles
Radio, Boots, Shoes, Hosiery, etc. Just think what this most
origonal scheme means to you. That money you are expending
week after week, soon becomes Shillings and Pounds, when
with a small weekly addition you can certainly benefit yourself.
Any further information we shall be only too pleased to give
you. Why not talk it over next time we call, or pay us a visit
to

ALDERTONS
(Reg; No. 389872)
793 ST. ALBANS ROAD
WATFORD HERTS.

**NOTE:- We claim to be the only libr-
arians offering such a generous
proposition to the public.**

As public libraries today are increasingly concerned with income generation, let us hope that
they do not go the way of this private library…

The reading room at North Watford Library, which opened in December 1937. A prominent 'Silence' sign sets the atmosphere.

Buildings in Church Street, including the old workhouse used before Shrodells in Vicarage Road. They were all demolished to make way for the car park between 1958 and 1960.

The Watford Board of Guardians and staff in 1929 outside the chapel attached to the workhouse and infirmary in Vicarage Road. The institution was intended for 280 inmates, and by this date the emphasis was more on medical relief. One local newspaper had a regular column, 'Bumbledom', which ridiculed the Guardians' activities. 'For many years the Guardians

have been content to go on pottering – adding to their buildings first in one direction, then another, only to make confusion worse confounded. At one time they discovered they had no dining hall for the poor people. They at once built one at the end close up to the bake-house windows, leaving the bake-house and kitchen in darkness.'

Building the chimney of Watford's refuse destructor in 1904. Watford was the only town in Hertfordshire to have a destructor and it showed great environmental responsibility. The heat produced from the furnace raised steam to pump the town's sewage to the sewage farms at Holywell and Cassio Bridge. The clinker by-product was sold to neighbouring councils for road foundations, concrete and filtration beds – this was ninety years ago!

The accounts section at the Town Hall, c. 1950.

Watford Police outside their station in King Street. The station, which opened in 1889, included eight cells for prisoners, an exercise yard, offices for police and magistrates, residential quarters for the Superintendent and other men, married and unmarried, and stabling for horses. It closed in 1940 and subsequently became a public house, aptly named the Robert Peel.

The architects' department at the Town
Hall, c. 1950.

LANCHESTER RICKARDS & LUCAS *Architects*, 47 Bedford Square W.C.1

DUNN, WATSON & CURTIS GREEN, *Architects*, 35 Lincoln's Inn Fields, London, W.C.

H. V. ASHLEY & WINTON NEWMAN, F.R.I.B.A., *Architects*, 14 Gray's Inn Square London W.C.

Typical semi-detached house plans from
'Municipal Watford and its Housing
Scheme', a booklet dating from 1920, in
which the borough stated its intention to
build 2,000 new houses. The main scheme
was at Harebreaks, where most of the houses
were to be constructed by Charles Brightman
& Sons. See also the photograph on p. 68.

BOROUGH OF WATFORD.
COAL PERMIT.

Holder's Signature and Address   *Registered No. of Holder*

....

....

INSTRUCTIONS. The Holder must enter above Number and Coal Merchant's
Name on Coupon, and hand to him when obtaining a supply.

Coupons are only available for date indicated, and are not transferable.

No further Coal may be acquired if householder's stock exceeds 5 cwts., or in
case of coke 10 cwts.

Permit for 1 cwt of Coal, and 2 cwts. of Coke, for two weeks ending January 1st, 1927.	Permit for 1 cwt. of Coal, and 2 cwts. of Coke, for two weeks ending December 4th, 1926.
HOLDER'S No.	HOLDER'S No.
COAL MERCHANT.	COAL MERCHANT.

Coupons for coal issued by the borough during the General Strike.

Outside the Fire Station in the High Street – but what is the occasion, and who is the sailor in the centre?

The Law on the streets of Watford. Shops, including George Longley's drapers, had to be boarded up when disappointment at the postponement of the Coronation celebration in 1902 turned to anger and destruction.

Henry West, who died in 1927 aged eighty-five, had held the joint office of Town Crier and Corn Exchange superintendent, following in his father's footsteps. He was also chief organ blower at St Mary's for fifty-five years.

Callow Land Girls' School in 1912. The girls look as if they have been told to wear their best frocks for the photograph.

Boys and girls eating their meals, segregated from each other at the London Orphan Asylum, *c.* 1908. There were nearly 500 resident pupils at this date.

Tennis courts in the girls' playground at the London Orphan Asylum. The instructions given to a girl leaving in 1912 included the advice: 'Be grateful to your benefactors and faithful to your friends. Be kind and charitable to the poor, remembering what has been done for you. Always suppress every emotion of anger, revenge, envy and covetousness and strive to do unto others as you would they should do unto you.'

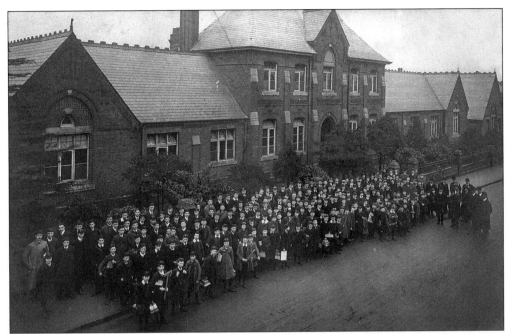

Boys 'clutching books and other impedimenta' from the Endowed School (Grammar School) in Derby Road on the march to their new premises in Rickmansworth Road, 23 February 1912. The girls had already moved into their new school in Lady's Close five years before. The school magazine described the change, 'Outside, no dirty gravelled playground, but acres of grassland with fine old trees, which promise grateful shade in the cricket time of year.'

Watford Grammar School. The Head Master's Room

The headmaster of the Boys' Grammar School for thirty years, W.R. Carter, in his study around 1913. Note the absence of such devices as a telephone, fax machine and computer – there is just a giant waste-paper basket.

Watford Grammar School. View from the field.

The new premises of the Boys' Grammar School, probably during its first year. At the opening ceremony one dignitary stated that he looked on the school 'as an instrument for fashioning Englishmen'.

In 1912 Watford Central School, the Higher Elementary section of Alexandra School, moved into Derby Road premises vacated by the Boys' Grammar School. Pupils started at the Central at the age of twelve and remained there for four years. In 1921 a Pupil Teachers' Centre was established there, which later specialized in domestic economy. Central Primary School now occupies the buildings.

GISBURNE HOUSE SCHOOL.

Gisburne House in Gammons Lane was a preparatory school from at least 1891 until 1910, 'a favourite prep school for the Public Schools and the Navy'. Later it became an industrial school for girls, run by the London County Council, and in the 1950s became a children's home.

Not only boys' schools had officer training corps. Here the Watford Girls' Grammar School corps is in step in the playground in March 1943.

And finally, two views of classes at Cassiobury Junior School, which opened in 1951. Originally the school was for both juniors and infants, but a new infants' school opened in 1968.